PEOPLE IN COSTUME

The 1930s and 1940s

JENNIFER RUBY

1930

1947

B.T. Batsford Ltd · London

1940

1930

First published 1995
© Jennifer Ruby 1995

Typeset by Goodfellow & Egan Ltd, Cambridge
and printed in Hong Kong by Colorcraft Ltd
Published by
B.T. Batsford Ltd
4 Fitzhardinge Street
London W1H 0AH

A CIP catalogue record for this book is available from the
British Library

ISBN 0 7134 7216 2

CONTENTS

1930

INTRODUCTION

In the 1930s, ladies' fashions were long, slim and elegant. Hats and gloves were worn for almost every occasion and a wealthy woman might change her outfit several times a day depending on her various activities. For those who were not so rich, the new chain stores provided inexpensive fashion. Many women copied the styles and make-up of the film stars they saw at their local cinema.

Men were always smart and were rarely seen outside the house without a jacket and hat. This was more to do with being respectable than fashionable as even poor men wore jackets, soft caps and mufflers (scarves).

During the Second World War, clothes had to become more practical. Men mostly wore uniforms and women wore plain outfits with square military-look shoulders. As in the First World War, many women took on men's work while the men were away fighting. This meant that more women began to wear trousers. As material became scarce, the government introduced clothes rationing. Decorative details on clothes such as pocket flaps and trouser turn-ups disappeared because they were considered to be a waste of cloth. People were encouraged to keep and mend their old clothes rather than buy new ones.

1937

After all these restrictions, women loved the 'New Look' launched by the French designer Christian Dior in 1947. This brought back a more feminine shape to women's clothes.

Let us now meet a soldier from the Second World War.

1945

'Hello, my name is Jack. I am an infantryman and I am fighting in France. This is my uniform and on my back I am carrying a shovel and a pack which contains my mess tin, emergency rations, a knife, fork and spoon, a cardigan, socks and a washing kit.

I have returned from France in order to take you on a journey through the 1930s and 1940s so that you can meet different characters and study the clothes they are wearing.

We will begin by visiting a large elegant country house in 1930.'

Jack

THE 1930s: IN THE COUNTRY

Alicia lives in a large house in the country with her husband Richard and several servants. They live a full and varied life with lots of different activities and tend to change their clothes several times a day.

Here you can see Alicia telephoning her friend Rachel in order to invite her to afternoon tea.

It is fashionable for ladies to have a long, slim, elegant shape. Alicia is wearing a dress which emphasizes this. She is carrying her engagement diary under her arm.

On the opposite page you can see Alicia and Rachel enjoying tea together in Alicia's study. Rachel is wearing a soft cap and a floral print dress and Alicia has on a plain dress with a contrasting V shape inserted at the neckline. Both ladies have high-heeled shoes.

Look at the items displayed in the bureau. Do they tell you anything about how Alicia spends her spare time?

Alicia

Rachel

Alicia

AT A POLO MATCH

Alicia and Rachel's husbands, Richard and Peter are keen polo players and sometimes the ladies go along to watch.

This is a wonderful excuse for them to dress up in their elegant gowns and matching hats and shoes. Here they are, pictured with another friend, Caroline.

Can you see the men in the background? They are immaculate in wide-topped white breeches and polished polo boots.

Caroline

EVENING WEAR

Here are Richard and Peter enjoying a drink together before a dinner party. Wealthy men always change into evening dress and Richard is wearing an evening jacket with tails, a white waistcoat and bow tie and trousers with a silk braid down the outside leg. Peter has on a dark suit with a waist-coat and bow tie.

Alicia and Rachel are dressed in long backless evening gowns.

Richard

Peter

Rachel

Alicia

ANYONE FOR TENNIS?

Alicia and Richard play a lot of tennis with their friends. On the left, you can see them arriving at Rachel and Peter's home for an afternoon of tennis. Can you describe their outfits?

After playing they will relax at the house in casual and stylish outfits like those pictured on this page.

MENSWEAR

Richard is a solicitor. Here he is in his business suit. His jacket is double-breasted and his trousers are quite wide and have turn-ups.

On the right he has changed into a different suit and overcoat for a night out with Alicia. Notice how slim Alicia's clothes make her look. There was a fashionable saying in the 1930s which was 'You can never be too slim or too rich'!

Richard

Richard

Alicia

LINGERIE

Alicia and Rachel wear very glamorous underwear and night-wear which is usually made of silk or satin.

On the right Rachel is wearing a silk dressing gown. On the far right, Rachel and Alicia are modelling a nightdress and petticoats.

Rachel

THE INFLUENCE OF HOLLYWOOD

Cinema-going became very popular during the 1930s and many women copied the styles and make-up of their favourite stars. Glamorous film stars of the 1930s included Marlene Dietrich, who started a fashion for feather boas and plucked eyebrows, and Joan Crawford, who was famous for her 'rosebud lips'.

Marlene Dietrich in the veiled hat and fox fur that she wore for her film 'Desire'

Joan Crawford in a black suit designed for her by Adrian, a top Hollywood designer

Here is Alicia in a long evening gown. She is wearing heavy make-up (called 'pancake' make-up) and bright lipstick. She has plucked her eyebrows to a thin line.

Try to find pictures of more Hollywood film stars from the 1930s and 1940s and look at the clothes they are wearing.

Alicia

HOME DRESSMAKING

We will now move forward to the year 1936 and visit Elizabeth who lives in the village near to Alicia and Richard's country house.

Elizabeth is not as wealthy as Alicia, so she makes most of her clothes herself. In this picture she is wearing a floral print dress with a detachable collar. She sent away for the pattern and material for this dress and it cost her 5s 9d which is about 28p in today's money!

On the opposite page you can see her with her friend Christine. Elizabeth is wearing a blue cotton overall over a yellow dress and Christine has on a red pinafore dress.

Women do not do as much dressmaking today as they used to. Why do you think this is?

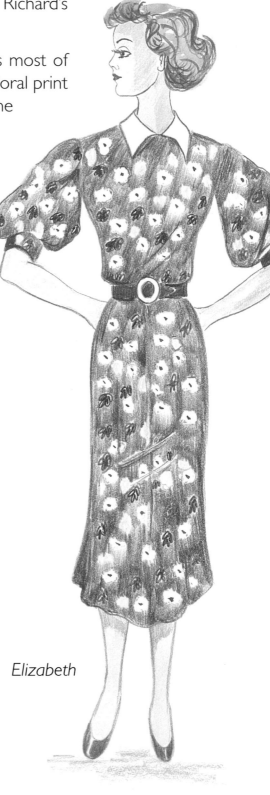

Elizabeth

Elizabeth

Christine

EVACUEE CHILDREN

To be evacuated means to be moved from a place of danger to a place of safety. In 1939, when the Second World War started, three and a half million children were moved from London and other big cities into the countryside where they would be safe from the threat of German bombing. Each child was assigned to a family with whom they lived.

Elizabeth and Christine have decided to take some evacuee children into their homes and have gone to the station to meet them.

Peter

Shirley

Marcia

The children have their belongings with them in pillowcases or suitcases and have name tags around their necks. One little boy, Peter, is being fitted with a new gas mask.

Two sisters, Shirley and Marcia, are waiting anxiously for instructions on where to go. Their mother was upset about them leaving home and has put a label on the girls which reads, 'please do not separate', in the hope that Shirley and Marcia will at least have each other when they are given their temporary home and family.

The children's clothes are very simple. Can you describe them? What do you think it would feel like to be sent away from home like this?

THE 1940s: LONDON

Now we will move forward to the year 1942 and to London, where people are suffering badly from the effects of the war. Many things are in short supply and are being rationed.

Catherine

Clothes are one of the things that are rationed. This means that everyone is given coupons which they have to give up when they buy garments. People can not buy too many clothes as the coupons soon run out.

The Utility Scheme also affects the clothes people can buy. This scheme limits the amount of cloth used in the making of garments. Clothes made under this scheme carry the label CC 41 and are very simple in style. For example, men's jackets are single breasted and have no pocket flaps and their trousers have no turn-ups. Women's dresses are shorter and close fitting.

Jennifer

On the left you can see Catherine in a Utility-style dress and a turban on her head. Jennifer and Susan are wearing Utility suits. The shoulders on all three garments have a square 'military' look, reflecting the war.

Utility clothes were not unattractive, but women felt that it was difficult to be original with the restrictions that were imposed.

Susan

PRACTICAL SOLUTIONS

Wartime conditions demanded practical, comfortable and hard-wearing clothes. Here is Catherine in a shelter suit (or siren suit) which keeps her warm when she has to spend the night in an air-raid shelter.

Stockings are in very short supply and on the opposite page you can see Jennifer having fake stockings painted on to her legs before she goes to a dance. Her friend Susan is wearing a tight fitting Utility jacket with padded shoulders and a straight, plain skirt. Jane has on a floral print dress that she has made herself.

All three girls have their hair in curls like sausages.

Catherine

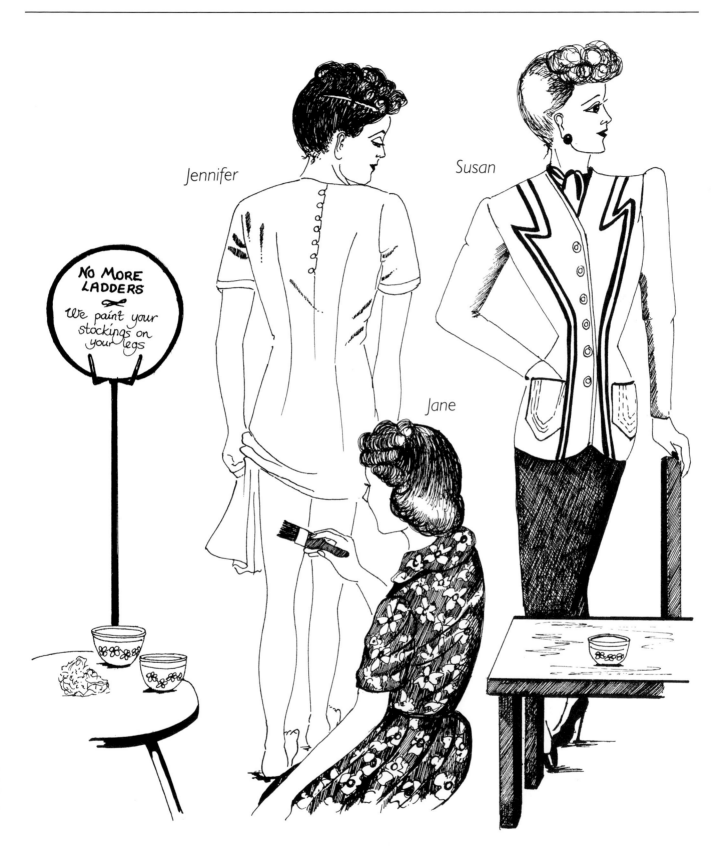

NON-UTILITY STYLES

Alison

Margaret

Doreen

During the war, 85 per cent of the clothes made were Utility but the remaining 15 per cent were free from restrictions. The 'free' clothes were in great demand but it is interesting that they were not very different in shape from the Utility styles.

Alison, Margaret and Doreen are having afternoon tea at an expensive restaurant. They are wearing non-Utility dresses with matching hats. Margaret (centre), has a long fur stole and a handbag to match her dress.

In contrast to war-torn Europe, America was a fashion haven where glamorous and stylish clothes were readily available. Alicia has just returned from a visit to America and is wearing an outfit that she bought there. It consists of a petrol-blue jacket, a brick-red blouse with matching skirt and hat and a brown leather handbag. She also has on a gold choker and matching earrings.

Alicia

WOMEN IN UNIFORM

Susan

During the Second World War many women joined the armed forces as Auxiliaries*. They looked after operations at home while the men fought abroad

Susan has joined the ATS (Auxiliary Territorial Service), which is the women's branch of the army. She is wearing her khaki uniform which consists of an army jacket, a skirt, a shirt, a tie and a peaked cap. Opposite, you can a see a poster advertising the ATS. This poster was banned by the Prime Minister, Winston Churchill, who said it made army life look too glamorous.

Susan's friend Jennifer has joined the Women's Land Army. She is working on a farm in the country as there is a shortage of farm workers. Her uniform consists of a brown felt hat, khaki breeches, a shirt and tie, a green jersey, woollen socks and stout shoes.

Catherine has become an air-raid warden. You can see her pictured in her tin hat. Can you find out what her duties might be?

*An auxiliary is a person or thing that supports or supplements something.

Poster for the Auxiliary Territorial Service (ATS)

Female air-raid warden

Women's Land Army

MEN AT WAR

Donald, Jeremy and Roger are fighting in the war. Donald is a tank man and is wearing a one-piece tank overall called a 'pixie suit'. If you compare this with the siren suit on page 26 and the 'dickie suits' on page 45 you will see how military uniforms influenced fashion.

Jeremy is a Commando. He is often sent on very dangerous missions. He has to remove his cap badge when he is on a raid. Why do you think this is?

Roger is an officer in the RAF and is wearing a leather fur-lined flying jacket, a blue-grey uniform and fur-lined boots.

Can you find some pictures of other uniforms from the Second World War?

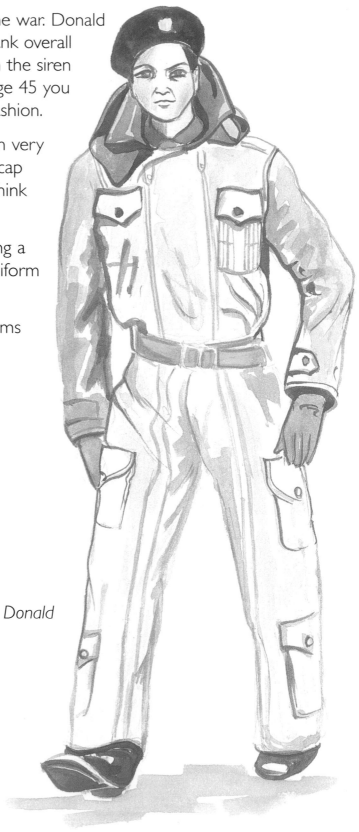

Donald

Jeremy

Roger

AT A DANCE

The jitterbug was a dance that arrived from America in 1942. It was very popular as energetic dancing was a great outlet for people's frayed nerves!

Susan

John

Susan and John are dancing the jitterbug at their local community hall. Susan is wearing a fitted jacket that she has made herself, a plain woollen skirt and low-heeled shoes. John is wearing a Utility suit. You can see that it has no pocket flaps or trouser turn-ups.

Jennifer and Catherine are also at the dance. They are wearing smart blouses and plain skirts and have their hair done in upswept styles. Once again, there is a 'square' look to the girls' shoulders. This is like the square shoulders on military uniforms.

Jennifer

Catherine

QUEUING FOR FOOD

As the war dragged on, food became scarce and women spent a long time queuing for their food rations. Here are some women waiting patiently to buy fish and chicken. What are they wearing? Can you write a tea menu for the tea shop next door?

MAKING DO

As everything was in such short supply during the war years, people had to use their imaginations to make things last or go further. There was even a government poster called 'Make Do and Mend' which encouraged women to mend their old clothes rather than buy new ones. Here is Susan in a suit that she has made herself by converting an old coat. She is also wearing a blouse which has a matching scarf. She made these from an old dress.

On the opposite page you can see a group of wealthy ladies attending a cookery class at a London hotel.

These women have lost their servants to the factories and are learning how to cook for themselves. The chef and his assistant are teaching them how to save on food.

Notice that all the women in the class are wearing hats and that their dresses all have the square-shouldered look.

What were some of the ways of saving bread?

Susan

THE NEW LOOK

In February 1947, Christian Dior, a French designer, launched his 'New Look' fashions. His designs had narrow shoulders, pinched-in waists and long flowing skirts. They looked very feminine after the military styles of the war years. You can imagine how much the women loved them after all the restrictions of the Utility fashions.

Here you can see Jennifer, Susan and Catherine wearing some 'New Look' fashions.

Jennifer

Catherine

Susan

HATS

One item of clothing that was not rationed during the war was the hat. This meant that in order to be original with their outfits, many women wore striking and unusual hats. On these two pages you can see examples of styles from the 1930s and 1940s.

1939

1939

1945

1941

1946

1944

Headscarves and turbans were seen everywhere during the war years

CHILDREN'S CLOTHES

Children's clothes were quite simple and comfortable during the 1930s and 1940s. Here are some examples of children's outfits. You could refer back to pages 22 and 23 and study what the evacuee children are wearing.

1934

'Dickie suits'

1940

ACCESSORIES

Now that we have finished our journey through the 1930s and 1940s you can test your skill. Look at the accessories pictured on these two pages and by looking at the dates, see if you can decide which character in the book each belongs to.

man's waistcoat, 1949

man's bowler hat, 1948

man's tweed country hat, 1940

mug

mess tin

1940

jackknife

lady's long embroidered glove, 1940

lady's shoe, 1943

1939: spectacles, lipstick, matching nail varnish, canvas bag

lady's platform sandal, 1938

lady's shoe with thick crepe rubber sole, 1949

man's shoe, 1936

lady's evening bag, 1934

lady's powder compact, 1933

man's suspender belt worn around the calf to hold up the sock, 1933

lady's hair clip, 1937

man's evening waistcoat, 1933

man's suede shoe, 1948

INDEX AND GLOSSARY